Contents

Introduction

If you are interested in learning a new foreign language, then this challenge is for you. Over the next 30 days, not only will you learn and make great progress in your language of choice but you will also learn the skills, techniques and tricks to insure that you make your way to language fluency in the quickest amount of time and more importantly, you will learn your new language without it ever feeling like a bore!

Additionally, you will gain the habit of studying your language each and every day which is a very important part of the process of learning a foreign language. Foreign languages are best learnt a little bit each and every day rather than large chunks every once in a while.

By following this 30 day schedule, you will get used to studying your new language day after day and will be able to continue studying even after you have completed the 30 day schedule.

In this way, after completing this 30 day course, you will have a great number of tools to help you learn your new language as well as the language studying habit installed so that you can continue your studies day after day until you have reached the level of proficiency in your language at which you feel comfortable.

I know that it will probably be tempting for you to simply look through each day right now and see what is stored there, but I would recommend not doing that. As I mentioned above, one of the great bonuses you will get out of doing this course is the habit of learning a language each and every day. So, although you may really want to just look through the entire contents of the course right now, it is best to wait until each day to do the exercises so that you can build up this habit of learning a new language which will ultimately carry you through to fluency.

Are you ready to begin your new language life? Great! Continue to "Day 1" and let's go.

You may be serious about starting this challenge and getting on the road to fluency in your new language or you may be wondering what this challenge is exactly about. In either case, you are about to learn a few mind switches that will enhance your language learning.

To insure the success of this challenge and your success in learning a new language, make a commitment right now for the next 30 days to do all of the exercises outlined in this plan. If you already know that you have some big change coming up in your life, such as if you are moving your home or changing jobs, this may not be the best time to begin a new project. If this is the case, simply bookmark this page and come back when you are ready.

If, however, you are ready to learn, then commit now and realize that for the next 30 days, you will be adding a new language to your life. If it helps you, write down your commitment on a piece of paper and tape it near your computer or simply stop and take the next 5 minutes to think about what this commitment will mean in your life.

It is very important that you be honest with yourself and seriously commit to this language change in your life. The more seriously you consider it, the more successful you will be.

So, why 30 days? You may have heard that it takes 30 days to install a new habit. This challenge is to help you do just that, give you the tools and techniques that you can use to be successful in learning your new language. After 30 days, you will have learned a great deal in your new language, but more importantly you will have installed the habit of language learning and you will have everything you need to continue on to even greater language fluency in the future.

Today, the most important task is to sit back right now and visualize yourself taking the time to enjoy learning a new foreign language over the next 30 days. Imagine vividly reading, learning, speaking and understanding your language. Focus on yourself improving your language skills over the next 30 days for at least 5 minutes. Even if you do not know a single word in your language yet and do not know how you will learn, simply focusing on the process of learning is enough.

Did you take the time and energy to focus on your language success? Great! Now, if you have a language learning book, audio program or some other material, open it or listen to it and learn one word or phrase in your new language. If you do not have any materials, you can go to Google and search for phrases in your language and find one there.

Today, you have made a commitment to your language success and created the right attitude. You have also learned your first bit in the new language. Good job!

N ow that you created the right attitude towards your language learning yesterday, you can begin to get familiar with your new language.

It is easier for your mind to grasp familiar objects than foreign ones.

For example, look at the two sentences below.

Hi, my name is Fred. How are you today?

Xop iw yidkl kiii lslqc oppli slvjjo oplzaiw.

If I covered up these two sentences and then asked you to repeat them back to me, you could probably repeat back the first one with 100% accuracy. The second one would be a bit more difficult. Most people probably wouldn't be able to remember anything from the second sentence a day or two from now whereas the first sentence would come back much more easily.

Why? It's simply that you have had more exposure to the first sentence and you are familiar with it. It is easier for your mind to grasp it.

Likewise, when you are confronted with your new language, your mind is going to be unfamiliar with it. The shapes and sounds of the words are going to be different and it will take some time for your mind to get used to them.

So today, you are going to get used to your new language.

First, let's start with text. Go to wikipedia.org and enter into the portal for the language you are trying to learn. For the next 10 to 20 minutes, simply scan over the text. You can try clicking through to different pages. Try reading quickly and then try reading slowly. Even if you do not understand a single word, the important part is to get your mind used to this new language.

As you read over the text, try to get used to the shapes and forms of the words, notice patterns in terms of repeated words or series of letters that seem to pop up together again and again. Compare the language to English... do the words seem longer in general? Shorter? Are there more consonants? More vowels?

If the language you are studying does not use the roman alphabet like English, take note of the way the script looks and flows. Think about how it differs from the roman alphabet that English uses and see if you can discern any patterns or symbols that come up again and again.

After going through a lot of text very quickly, your mind will begin to feel more comfortable with the new language and you will find it easier to pick up the language later as you begin to learn the details and specifics of words.

Now, you will spend the next 10 to 20 minutes getting accustomed to the sounds of the new language. You can either go to a video site like YouTube or go to Google and search for audio in your language. Simply find a video of any kind and listen to the language. Again, it is not important to understand what is being said. What is important is to simply allow yourself to accept the new sounds and rhythms.

After listening for a while, try to get a sense of the language. Does it sound rougher or softer than English? Do you notice any strange sounds that don't seem to occur in English? Are there certain rhythms or patterns in the pitch that you can hear?

After you have completed these two exercises, you can now go back to your language learning material and learn two more words or phrases. Also take a look at the word or phrase you learned yesterday and see if there are any similarities. Do these words and phrases seem to conform to the sense you developed today of the language you are learning?

Today you developed a sense of your new language which is the background for the language landscape you will develop. You also got the opportunity to learn a few more concrete bits of the language!

Now that you have your attitude set right and a general sense of the language, you can begin to get more involved in learning specifics.

If you have a language textbook, book, audio program, software program or some other material that you really wish to use, go ahead and begin the first chapter, lesson or section. You can learn as much as you want and go as far in the program as you wish today. However, as soon as it begins to feel boring or feels like work that you do not want to do, just stop and put the book or program down. Ultimately, language learning is about your enjoyment, so never force yourself. Not only will it not feel good but it's not a very efficient way of learning, either.

If you have no language material to learn with, or if you are looking for some more practice or a different taste, you can look for many of the free language learning materials online. If you go to Google and search for language learning materials, you can often find free courses that will teach you the basics. If you are lucky enough, you may even be able to find a "podcast" which are audio lessons that you can download and listen to. In the beginning, you can use these free materials to begin learning the new language. Again, learn as much as you want but as soon as it begins to feel boring or like hard work, just stop. You can either try to find another program and switch over to that or simply rest for the day.

Today you began to get into the workings of the language, learning some of the concrete basics.

You will want to continue building your storehouse of words and phrases in your new language.

Since these are the basics, you can be sure that you will come across them again and again in your journey in your language. Words and phrases like "Hello", "How are you?" are language that you should make sure you can say without having to think twice. This is the language that you will use when you run into someone who speaks the language natively or if you happen to go to the country where it is spoken. Make sure you can say these phrases effortlessly so that you don't end up floundering when the opportunity to meet a native speaker presents itself to you!

Additionally, you will begin to learn the basics of grammar. You will learn the present tense and other simple workings of the language. If you do not understand the grammar at first, do not worry. It is actually easier to learn the grammar through experience of using the language. So even if it does not seem clear to you now, simply recognize that it is there and move on. Sometime in the future, it will come back to you and make sense.

Today focus on building up more of the basic vocabulary and grammar structure as you can. Try to push yourself, it is okay to move on even if you do not understand or remember 100% of the material. In fact, you will find that it will be easier to remember 100% of the material if you become advanced and then look back so continue on until you reach the point where you begin to feel bored or no longer feel good about studying the language. You may find that in order to keep the language interesting, you have to go quicker, moving through your language material at a fast rate. This is perfectly fine, you can always go back and review or move through it quickly again tomorrow in order to better retain the language.

Today you really got the basics of beginning conversation down so that you can say the words or phrases without thinking twice. You also made good headway in the basics becoming familiar with more vocabulary and grammar.

Begin by reviewing what you have learned over the last few days.

Then, imagine if you were to walk outside your house and run into a native speaker of the language you are trying to learn. Think of exactly what you would say.

Would you be able to introduce yourself? Ask your new friend where he or she is from? Could you talk about why you want to learn the language? Could you express that you are just a beginner or that you don't speak much of the language?

It's likely that even from the learning you have done over the past few days, you know a few phrases that could help you out. Maybe you know how to say "Hello" or "How are you?". It's also likely that you don't know all the vocabulary or grammar structure to fully say what you would want to say to a native speaker. Perhaps you have great respect for the literature or movies of the country where the language is spoken and don't know how to say "movie" or "book"!

Whatever the case may be, take some time and look in a dictionary to find the words that you need in order to carry on this conversation with a native speaker. You may find that using a phrase book can be particularly useful in getting useful phrases for introductions or asking about the native speaker or talking about yourself.

As you imagine this conversation with the native speaker in your head, try to write down and figure out some of the things you would say. It's very likely that you will have to simplify what you want to say because you don't possess enough vocabulary or grammar structure. This is perfectly fine and is actually a useful skill when learning a new language. You should get used to being able to find new ways of expressing yourself with the vocabulary and grammar you have.

Don't worry too much about being 100% absolutely correct and also do not try to memorize the phrases that you have created. You only want to memorize phrases that you know for sure are correct in terms of vocabulary usage and grammar.

The purpose of this exercise is to prepare yourself for a conversation you may have if you ever bump into a native speaker. Since language is about communication, this is one of our top priorities!

After spending some time on this exercise, make sure you make some more progress in your language learning material, learning new words and grammar. Also quickly review the first parts that you have already learned to make sure they do not slip your mind.

Today you thought about how to express yourself in your new language to a native speaker and also began to learn the skill of expressing yourself even when you cannot say exactly what it is you want to say. You also made more progress in your language learning materials gaining even more phrases to your language arsenal.

R emember that imagined conversation you did yesterday? Well, now it's time to put it into action!

You are going to use the chat site "SharedTalk" to communicate with a real, live native speaker in the language you are learning.

If you haven't heard of it, just go to www.SharedTalk. com. It is a chat site that can be used for both voice chat and text chat. If you don't have a microphone already, you will want to buy one in order to speak. Most laptops however have a microphone built in! If you don't have a microphone or are too shy for now, you can just communicate with the native speaker through text chat.

Go to sharedtalk.com and go to the search function then simply search for people in the country where your language is spoken. Many names will come up of people who are interested in talking to new friends. Simply choose one you think looks interesting and send them a message!

You can either start off by saying "Hello" in your new language or explaining to them that you are trying to learn their language and ask them for help.

If the person is not there, is not agreeable or only wants to speak in English, you can always go back to the search function and try someone else. There's no need to stick with someone who does not want to help you.

Your conversation will probably be brief but that is okay. If the other person uses a word or phrase that you don't understand, you can either take the time to look it up in a dictionary at that moment or tell them in their language that you don't understand and ask them to explain. If they speak English, they may be able to give you a translation. In any case, if the conversation becomes too difficult or too confusing, you can simply tell your conversation partner that you are sorry but you need to go. Afterwards, while you have more time, you can look up the words you didn't know and begin to understand the conversation.

If you are feeling particularly brave and already know a bit of the language, you can ask your new conversation partner to voice chat with you. Voice chatting is quicker than text chatting and doesn't allow you as much time to look things up in a dictionary but it is definitely good practice for speaking and listening. Two actions which you will definitely need to be good at if you want to learn your language!

After you have talked to a native speaker in the language, make sure you continue your studies in the language material you have. You should be making progress each day, learning new vocabulary and grammar structure. Now that you have spoken to someone and have the possibility to talk to a native speaker whenever you like, it should give you an extra boost to remember that vocabulary and also learn new phrases so that you can better express yourself.

Of course it is hard to communicate with a native speaker now, but if you continue on, it will only become easier. Additionally, the practice of attempting to communicate is good learning in itself.

Today you had your first conversation with a native speaker in your new language. Congratulations! You are already learning to communicate and you made more progress in your studies.

T hink back about yesterday's conversation with the native speaker, was there any new vocabulary or was there anything you wanted to say but didn't know the words for? If so, make sure you look up all these words to learn them. This way, the next time you encounter a native speaker, you will be ready and can go even further in the conversation.

Also take a look at your language learning material. Is it teaching you material that you find useful? It is an unfortunate fact that many language learning books and programs teach you items which are not so useful in your life. If this is the case, you will either want to try and find new material or you will want to make sure that you have other sources for learning. Also, don't worry so much about memorizing vocabulary 100% that you don't think you will use. There's no use in learning words like "potato" when you are first starting out since the chances that you will come across this word in a beginning conversation are very slim. On the other hand, if you are a chef, you may very well want to learn "potato" and every other kind of food word that you can since you will likely find yourself in conversations about food.

Continue to make progress in your language materials but also begin to actively learn what you think will be useful for you. Also make sure to take note and remember any words from your conversation yesterday or look up and write down any words that are important to you that you think may come up in a conversation like your hobbies, work or anything else related to your life.

At this point, you are better at using phrases in your arsenal to make basic conversation with a native speaker and you should have a good idea of the way a conversation will flow in your new language.

Today, you not only made more progress in your new language but you are also starting to take control of the language you learn since this is the language that will benefit you most in the future.

At this point, you should focus on two parts of your language learning. The first part should be focus on grammar and other grammatical structure of the language. This is the part of the language you need to understand if you want to differentiate between the past, present, conditional, etc. Textbooks, language programs and grammar explanations are perfect for covering this part.

The other part of your study should focus on building your vocabulary. This type of study should include texts that you find interesting. So, today, try to think of something that you could read in your new language that you would want to read.

You may actually already have something in mind to read as part of your goal for learning the language in the first place. Maybe you are interested in the literature and took up the study of the language to better understand it. Or perhaps you live in a community or country where the language you are trying to learn is spoken and you want to be able to read the signs and newspapers around you. If this is the case, then you probably already have some material in mind that you want to use.

If nothing springs to mind that you want to read in particular in your new language then think if you have a hobby or already have a topic that you enjoy reading in English. You can simply use that subject. Once you have the subject in mind that you want to explore in your new language. You can begin to find texts written about it. Good places to look for texts are either to begin by going to Wikipedia in your new language and searching for the topic, going to Google and searching for the topic or finding a newspaper online written in your language and searching for news articles about the topic.

Once you have a text ready that you are genuinely interested in reading and understanding, you can begin to read it. Of course, there is going to be a large number of words that you do not know. It may even be the case that you don't understand 99% of the words written. This is perfectly fine, simply begin to learn the words that come up.

It will be slow going at first but if you stay within your topic, you will begin to notice that certain words come up again and again. If you are reading about tennis, you might see words like "match", "serve", "win", etc. As you continue to read about your topic and you become more familiar with the words often used within it, your comprehension level will go up.

As for grammar, do not worry too much. Since you are still a beginner, there will probably be grammatical forms that come up that you do not understand. What you should do is recognize that those forms are there and maybe take note of them or see if you can see any patterns. For now, you can try to discern the meaning of the article from vocabulary.

In the coming days, you will be reading much text related to the topic of your choice in order to learn new vocabulary so be sure to choose a topic that you are truly interested in!

Today you learned to focus not only on grammar but enjoyable texts as well. Soon you will be increasing your vocabulary comprehension even more!

R emember how you found a text about a topic that interested you yesterday? If you haven't finished reading that text, then continue to read it. If you did happen to finish the text or will finish your current text sometime in the future, it is a good idea to find a similar text about the same topic.

As you continue to read similar articles and texts, you will have repetition of vocabulary which will serve to help you learn better. Additionally, you will have the fun experience of being able to recognize words that you know and begin to understand what is going on.

You should continue to learn grammatical structures from a language learning book or online tutorial if you find that it helps you. These resources will only help you in your comprehension. You may even have noticed that as you read your text and article, you have begun to recognize different grammatical forms and structures that you learned about.

Today you continued to make progress in real texts, learning new vocabulary related to a topic that interests you while also begin exposed to the real language you are learning!

Y ou will continue the same rhythm that you have developed in the last two days, reading texts that interest you. If you find that a text is too difficult or you have trouble staying focused on it, then simply leave it and find a new one. At no point should you feel that you are forcing yourself too much.

Continue to learn new vocabulary related to your topic from the texts that you are reading. You will also find that you are picking up some of the more common words in the language simply by reading the real article. In English, these words would be words like "the", "a", "of", "one".

If it interests you, you can also try to figure out some of the grammar forms that you come across. You can either try to look them up in your language learning material or search for a grammar tutorial online. If you have a book like "501 Language Verbs", you can look up the form in there as well as learn more about the verb tense in general.

Today you continued your acquisition of new vocabulary and began to take notice of different grammar structures, attempting to ascertain their meanings.

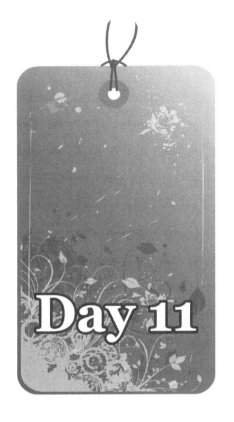

C ontinue your text reading today learning new vocabulary and attempting to recognize and understand some of the grammar structures you come across.

At this point, you may have developed a way of keeping track of the new words you come across. Maybe you have written them down somewhere.

If you don't have a way of keeping track of the words and simply look up the words then move on, you probably have noticed that you often end up looking up the same word again and again because you have forgotten its meaning by the time you come across it again.

For this reason, it is important to take note of the vocabulary in some way so that you can either study it later on or at least try to reinforce it in your mind. This way, you will have a better chance of remembering it the next time you come across it.

So today, as you continue your reading and learning of new vocabulary, try making note of the words you come across or make some sort of active effort to remembering them. Otherwise, you will find that you will lose much time in continually looking up the same words again and again.

Today you increased your vocabulary and considered a way to enhance your vocabulary retention.

T oday read your text making sure that you take note of the new words you come across.

Now that you have a way of looking at the words you have learned, you can use this as a motivational factor. If you have a list of words, it gives you a good way of seeing visually the progress you have made in the language so far. Also, you can keep track of how many new words you can pick up each day.

Of course, simply looking up the words and writing them down does not mean you will remember them in the future or that you have fully learned them, but it does give you a good starting point. In future days, I will give you some tricks to help you remember the vocabulary but for now, during your studies, make a point of trying to remember and learn the new vocabulary.

Since you will be getting a good bit of repetition in your reading and studying already, it should become easier to pick up the words. Just make sure to spend a little extra time on those words that always seem to slip through your mind.

From now on, you can continue your reading and your grammar studying while keeping track of the progress you've made in learning vocabulary. Use this as a motivational factor to keep you learning more!

I n your reading, you have probably come across a lot of material you do not understand. Maybe it's a word that does not appear in your dictionary or maybe it's a grammar structure you can't seem to find listed anywhere. Whatever the case may be, you either took note of this question or at least remember it. If you cannot recall any specific cases, then today during your reading, begin to write down or take note of any areas that you cannot understand.

After your reading, you will have a list of questions or problem points. The point of this list is to keep it handy for the next time you run into a native speaker. You can then look at your list and kindly ask the speaker to explain the meaning. Sometimes native speakers will be unable to explain grammar points or other terms to you since to them, it is just natural. If this is the case, then either move on to the next question or leave it for a later day.

So, what kind of native speaker do you ask these questions to exactly? If you are studying the language, you may have already made a friend who is fluent or speaks the language natively. If that is the case, you can simply bring up the questions whenever it is convenient.

However, if you do not have any friends or do not know anyone who speaks the language, you can easily make one on SharedTalk. In fact, you can go back and ask the same person who you had a conversation with on SharedTalk last week. If that person is not online or you want to meet someone new, you can always use the search function until you find who you are looking for.

You can even have multiple native friend speakers who you can ask questions to and receive great help in learning the language. You will find that many people are helpful and perfectly willing to help someone out who is trying to learn their language.

Today you increased your language comprehension and also became aware of a great language resource to help you out with problem spots: native language friends!

As always, you should continue your reading and reviewing of grammar but today, we're going to branch out a little more.

Today we will use YouTube to find interesting videos. YouTube is a great resource to find various language materials. You can search and watch for whichever type suits you the best.

If you are learning a language that is commonly learned by English speakers, you may find video projects that students have done for class or other types of work. These may be beneficial for you since the language ability will also probably be at the beginner level. However, be careful since because these are students who are also learning the language, it is likely that they will make mistakes! Additionally, their accents will probably be far from perfect.

On the other hand, you can try to find native materials. You can search for news clips, music videos or videos that native speakers have filmed of themselves speaking. Try watching a few different kinds of videos and find the type that is most interesting to you.

There will be, of course, much material that you will not understand but this is perfectly fine. Simply by listening to the speech, your mind is becoming more used to it and this will only lead to better comprehension in the future. Even if you pick up only a word or two here and there, this is far better than when you had first started out in the language and knew nothing.

Today you continued on in your language reading and vocabulary building as well as found some new resources on YouTube to have fun in the language and get even more exposure!

T oday is Day 15 which means you are half way through the challenge! Congratulations!

Of course, you will still want to continue your reading and reviewing today, as well! However, today we are also going to step back and take a look at your language studying habits up until this point.

Now that you have some experience in learning your language, you may have noticed that certain time periods or times of the day work better for you. Maybe you have noticed that you enjoy studying in two chunks of time, once in the morning and once in the evening. Or maybe you have never tried studying for two chunks of time and decide that you want to try that.

Whatever the case may be, evaluate your studying habits and try to emphasize the ones that make you the most productive. There is no point in wasting time trying to study at a time that is inconvenient for you.

You should also consider challenging yourself. If you have gotten comfortable studying for a period of time, try lengthening that period of time or adding another small study session sometime in the day, maybe right before you go to sleep.

Also consider the way that you study the language. Do you read first and then study grammar? Or do you study grammar and then read later? Try switching up the order in which you do your studies.

Think about the number of words you are learning each day and how many of them you remember. If you have a long list but can't recall the words very well, say, less than 80%, you may want to add an additional 5 minutes at the end of your study session to go over all your vocabulary in order to reinforce those words' meanings.

The point is that you should be trying to always improve and better the way you study and the way you learn the language. In this way, you will keep yourself efficient and learn even faster.

Today you made it half way through the challenge learning a good deal of your new language. You also considered the way you studied and are looking forward to trying some new challenges in the next half of the challenge!

Today try out some of the new challenges you created for yourself yesterday. If they seem to work and make you learn more, then keep them. If after a few days of trying something new, it doesn't seem to work very well, then adjust it or think up of another idea to keep improving.

Of course, today continue your reading in material and collecting new vocabulary to learn. Since vocabulary is a major factor of learning any language, it makes sense to take a look at the way you learn vocabulary.

When trying to learn something like a new word, it becomes easier to learn it if you create lots of connections in your mind for it. This means that you shouldn't just look up the new word in a dictionary and write it down then try to look at it later to memorize it.

Instead, you should try to consciously think about the word and make any kind of connection that you are able to. For example, if you find a new word, think about any words that you know of that are similar. Especially if you are studying a language that is similar to English, you may want to think of English words that are similar. Additionally, you may also want to think about how the word is different from other words that you have already learned. By consciously activating your mind, you are taking large steps to insuring that you will remember the word later.

Also, another tip to help you remember new words is to consider the word in the context that you find it. Look very carefully at the sentence that the word appears in and think about the surrounding words. If you were to write that same sentence, do you think you would use the word the same way?

All of these questions and connections that you consciously make in your mind concerning a new word will help imprint it into your memory. Especially if you find yourself having trouble with one particular word that always seems to slip your mind, take a minute, sit down and try to create as many connections and ways of remembering the word in a minute's time. After you complete this task, the next time you encounter the word, you will find it is not so hard to remember it.

Today not only did you learn more of your language but you also improved your ability to remember and learn new vocabulary.

Keep up your work in your reading and also remember to take time to look over grammatical structure and learn new grammar points in your language.

You may find now that there are certain grammar points that are hard for you to remember. Maybe you confuse declensions for nouns or mix up verb tenses. Whatever the case may be, you will learn a way to deal with these tricky grammar situations.

The best way to conquer a grammar problem is to create a sample sentence that uses that grammar point. You can make the sentence as simple as you want or as creative as you want as long as you think you can remember it. The point is that you want to memorize this sentence to use as a blueprint for that grammar point.

By creating this one sample sentence that fully shows the grammar point, you may find that it already makes it easier for you to utilize and remember that point in the future. Additionally, you can use this sentence as a reference point if you start to stumble when trying to remember the grammar later. Eventually you won't even need to refer back to the sentence and the grammar will come naturally but for now if you ever find yourself having trouble, simply think back or recall the sentence you memorized and use it as a reference point to compare to the new sentence you are looking at.

If you ever have trouble with a certain grammar point again and again, then do what you do for troublesome vocabulary. Simply take a minute or two, sit back and try to create as many connections and thoughts about the grammar point as you can. If you want, you can try to look it up in a grammar book or try to find as many sample sentences that display the grammar as you can to fully impress the point in your mind.

Today you continued your language studies making more progress and also became aware of a way to handle problematic grammar.

As you continue to learn more and more vocabulary, you may have already developed your own techniques that work best for you in studying these new words.

Today you will learn another popular vocabulary learning technique that you can use if it seems to work well. This technique involves creating stories to help you learn the words. It is similar to the technique you learned before where you tried to create as many connections as possible to the word in that by creating a story for the word, you are also consciously choosing to think and create additionally information around the word to help you remember it.

The story technique simply involves you creating some story, no matter how fanciful, that includes all the elements of the word.

For example, in Japanese, the word for "foreign trade" is pronounced "boh – eh – key". So, to remember this word's meaning, you might create a story or an image in your head of the Japanese trading with other nations a "bow" and arrow for "a key". Thus you get all the elements of "trade", as well as the word's pronunciation "boh – eh – key".

As you can see, the stories and images do not have to make sense and in fact, they are sometimes easier to remember if they happen to be unrealistic. So, try to create whatever is most fanciful and easiest for you to remember.

In time, you will find that as you get more familiar with the word, these stories will drop off, so there is no need to worry about cluttering your mind with fanciful images. They are merely a technique to help you get the word into your memory for good.

Today you learned another technique to help you learn vocabulary faster and better and you also got further along in your language studies.

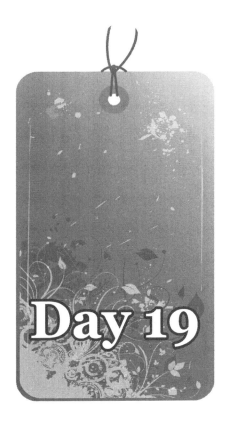

T oday your task is to revisit the exercise of creating a conversation that you might have with a native speaker. In the first week you may have found it difficult since you did not know many words or phrases in your new language. However, at this point, you have learned even more grammatical structure and have been exposed to many words in a subject that interests you through your reading.

The first conversation exercise involved creating a conversation that dealt with meeting a native speaker for the first time and introducing yourself. Think back to that conversation and see if there is any way you can improve it with any words or phrases that you have learned since then.

Now, take the conversation a bit further. Imagine that the native speaker asks you about an interest of yours or you happen to find that the native speaker is also interested in your hobby or interest. Create some dialogue concerning what you would say about your topic and think of different ways to express yourself using vocabulary that you have learned from your studies.

Remember, it is likely that you will not be able to say 100% what you wish to say. This is perfectly fine, simply try to find another way to express yourself in a way that is similar or close to what you want to say. This skill of expressing yourself in ways that may not be perfectly what you want because of your language limits is vital to speaking a new language. It will help you in the future when you may have to say something but don't have the time or ability to look up the word or grammar structure that you need.

Also, since you are still learning the language, it is likely that you will make mistakes. This is fine, too. Don't try to memorize your sentences or put any more effort into them after you have written them. If you desire, you can take the conversation to your native speaker friend that you made before and ask them to correct it or make suggestions. Then you can look at the natural sentences that your friend has created and memorize those in preparation of the future if you want.

Today you practiced the important skill of expressing yourself in your new language and also got the opportunity to use some of the new words and phrases you have been learning over the past few weeks.

C ontinue to do your reading, learning of new vocabulary and reviewing of grammatical structure.

Remember on the first day when you took the time to visualize your goals in learning the new language and made the commitment to learn your new language? Today you are going to revisit that.

Take five minutes and try to remember that time on Day 1 when you imagined what it would be like to learn the language. Then, take some more time and add anything else that you want to your vision or goal with the language. Do you see yourself taking a trip and being able to communicate effortlessly with locals? Do you see yourself being able to turn on the TV in the language and being able to understand what is going on without the aid of a dictionary? There are all kinds of experiences that you may desire so take some time and create a clear vision and goal of what it is that you want with your language.

When you have finally created the image that you want, you may want to write down a few sentences of words to give you something to look at in the future if you ever find that your motivation is beginning to slow down.

Additionally, now that you have studied the language for a few weeks, it is a good time to reflect on your previous goals and either make adjustments or recommit yourself to studying even harder and having even more fun in the language.

Remember that if something does not feel right or it seems like too much work when studying, that only means that you are not studying in the best manner for you. All you need to do is take five or ten minutes and think of a different way or option to study the language and then go out and try that. Eventually you will discover a material, way or technique that will best fit you and your needs.

Today you furthered yourself in your language and also re-envisioned your goals making them stronger in your mind.

Day 21

As always, make sure you are reading and collecting new vocabulary to learn. If you get tired of this, switch up the material to a new topic or find a different medium to read. For example, switch from reading newspaper articles to reading a fiction novel or switch from reading wikipedia to reading personal blogs.

When studying a language, it is important to remember some of the good things about the practice in order to keep you motivated. Firstly, you should consider the direct benefits that you expect the language to have in your life. You probably covered some of this yesterday when you envisioned your goals and what you eventually want out of the language. Think about how learning the language will help you in your career, personal life, on your travels or anywhere else.

Additionally, there are many other benefits that you may not have considered before. For example, the act of learning a new language is an intellectual process that is only good for your brain. You may consider it to be a mental work out that keeps your mind fit and healthy. Many studies have already shown that learning a second language actually prevents adults from developing neurological disorders like dementia and alzheimer's.

As you can see, not only do you get the direct benefits in your life but you will also get a host of indirect benefits in the form of mental sharpness, clarity and the prevention of mind disorders that obviously can cause a decline in quality of life.

Today you considered the benefits of learning a new language implanting in your mind the fact that language learning practice is good for your mental health. You also improved your language abilities today, too!

Day 22

After you have finished your daily reading and study of vocabulary, you are going to do an exercise to help you develop your abilities in the grammatical structure of the language.

If your language has verb tenses or other conjugations, you may find it difficult to choose the correct one when trying to form your own sentences. If this is the case, then take 10 minutes or more and focus simply on conjugating these verb tenses using a simple sample sentence like "I eat the bread" or "I go to the store".

You will want to conjugate this sentence in many ways depending on the form of your language and the differences it has. You may go from "I eat the bread" to "You eat the bread" to "We eat the bread" and so on. You may also want to change aspect or tense time-wise such as "I eat the bread" to "I ate the bread" to "I would eat the bread" and so on.

When you say each sentence, try to form a clear mental image or feeling in your mind of a situation where this might occur. It does not matter so much what the actual action is but rather try to focus on the feeling of that conjugation in terms of the relationship. For example, if you say "I eat the bread", try to emphasize in your mind the sense of "I" in relation to the part of the verb that conjugates and changes for this part. Do the same when you say "You eat the bread" but instead emphasizing the "you"ness in your mind. In this way, your mind will begin to correspond and create connections between that verb tense and the concept that you are expressing.

You may find this practice beneficial to you and want to do it every now and then in order to freshen the concepts or simply to practice them to make them more readily available.

Today you made further progress in learning new vocabulary and you also focused on grammatical structures forming them better in your mind allowing yourself in the future to use them with ease.

As you continue your vocabulary learning, you may consider creating some goals for yourself in order to push yourself to learn even more.

If you want, you can make a calendar and begin to keep a tally of all the words you collected and learned on that day. This way, you can measure your results and then perhaps tie rewards to them. For example, if there is a very interesting novel you want to read, you will tell yourself that you will allow yourself to read it once you have learned 1000 words in your language. If you are someone who likes chocolate, you may rewards yourself with a piece of chocolate once you have learned and reviewed 5, 10 or 20 words that day.

By creating goals and rewards like this, it helps motivate you to push yourself and try to learn more each day. However, don't try to push yourself too hard since you run the risk of trying to learn too many words and not being able to remember any of them later.

All in all, this is a fun practice to see your real results in the language. Additionally, being able to look back and see in real numbers the progress you have made is a great feeling that can only help to propel you on to learn even more.

Today you learned more language and you also considered making some goals for yourself to increase the number of words you learn and the rate at which you learn them.

Day 24

After you have finished doing your vocabulary collecting from your reading and your learning of new words, you are going to get more involved in listening to the language.

Now that you have some vocabulary under your belt, you can attempt to listen to the language and comprehend it.

One of the best ways you can go is to search for native radio casts in the language you are studying. Simply go to Google and search for radio in the language you are studying. You will find that there are many places where you can listen online for free to radio from that country where your language is spoken. This is great listening practice and you can also turn it on whenever you want even when you are not doing active language study and are just surfing the web, for instance.

Not only will this allow you to get more familiar with the sounds of the language which will lead to better comprehension in the future, but you will be pleased when you are able to pick out words here and there that you understand.

If you are able to, try to find radio stations that interest you or that are involved in a topic that you like. Another resource you can try to find is podcasts. Podcasts are simply audio files that people release on any number of topics. It may be possible that a native speaker is making a podcast online about a topic or hobby that you are pursuing. Try to search Google for such a podcast and if you can find one, great! This means that you will have a better chance of understanding the vocabulary since you have already been trying to learn these kinds of words through your studies up until this point. Additionally, it will give you the chance to learn more vocabulary related to a topic that you enjoy.

Today you furthered yourself in your language and also began to get more involved in the listening part of the language.

L ike yesterday when you went out to find a radio station or podcast in the language you are studying, today you are going to branch out some more. Remember that even as you go out to find new materials and places to practice your language, it is important that you continue your practice of finding new words and learning them. Make sure you review and do active learning each day. You can also do this practice in the new areas that you find in addition to your reading.

Today, you will branch out by going to Google and attempting to find other places where you can practice and learn the language. Some of the better and more interesting places to do this is to search for personal blogs written in the language you are studying or try to find a message board where native speakers are having real conversation. You can also look for study groups in the language you are studying where people help each other out.

Whatever it may be that you find, if you search, you will probably find something interesting and fun that will keep you engaged in the language and will probably teach you a thing or two in the language, as well.

As before, if you want, you can use these message boards and resources to learn new vocabulary and progress your active studying even further. Remember that textbooks, newspaper articles and similar materials are not the only places to learn the language. Real live conversations being held by native speakers are also great resources.

Today you actively studied more vocabulary and began to branch out into other areas to find places to use your language to further your understanding even more.

J ust like yesterday, today you are going to consider places where you can branch out but instead of these places being online, you are going to consider places outside.

Now, if you live in a small town and already know that there are no native speakers or anything related at all to your language anywhere near you, this may be difficult. However, if you live in an area with a sizeable number of people, especially a city, you may be surprised at what you can find.

You can try to go to your library and see if they have any language materials there. They most likely have language learning materials but also check to see if they have any books written in the language you are studying. Also, check to see if there are any supermarkets or stores related to the country where your language is spoken. These can be great places to go and not only immerse yourself in the culture of the language you are studying but you may be able to make a native speaker friend or two, as well.

Additionally, check to see if there is an embassy or some sort of cultural organization in your area for the language you are studying. If there is, they may host events of other programs including classes or places where you can learn the language. These can also be great places to make native speaker friends, as well as simply get the opportunity to practice your language skills.

Lastly, if you are in a city with a sizeable population of people from the country with the language you are studying, you may want to consider volunteering in some organization or group related to these people. This is a very good way to not only do some good but also make friends who speak the language and have experiences where you can practice it.

Today you furthered your language abilities and also thought about ways to go out and use your language which you will be doing in the near future.

Day 27

J ust as you found radio and audio online, it is time to add another fun resource that you can use to learn your language. Today you are going to try to find television online from the country where the language you are studying is spoken.

Especially if you are studying a language with a lot of speakers, you will find that it is very easy to find television online that you can watch for free. Although the quality may not be very good, this is a fun way to get exposed to the culture of the country and also improve your language comprehension.

Simply go to Google and search for the language you are studying and television. It may be difficult to find a free online broadcast if the language you are studying is not spoken by very many people. If this is the case, then simply try to find videos online at popular video sites like YouTube.

Watching television online is another resource you can use to improve your language abilities but always remember to do some active study, as well. That means actively finding words that you do not know and noting them down to learn later.

Today you found television, a new resource to help you along in your studies. You also improved your language abilities some more.

Day 28

T oday you are going to consider the question of "fluency". Fluency is a very tricky term in that there is no good way of defining it. Ultimately, what is considered "fluent" is really up to whoever is using it.

For you, however, you should think about fluency and what it means to you in your studies. How far do you want to go in your language? Do you want to be able to just make simple conversation or do you want to be able to read scholarly articles? Do you want to be able to just get the general gist of what is going on when you watch television or do you want to understand every word?

Asking these kinds of questions will help you focus your language studying efforts in the places where you want them. Also, you should remember that there will always be new material for you to learn in the language. How far you go in the language is really up to you and what you desire.

As you continue to learn new words and grammar, think about your fluency goal and how the words and grammar you are learning fit into reaching that goal. Remember that each word that you learn is another step to reaching that level. In this way, each second you spend studying the language is important.

You learned even more of your language today and also considered the term "fluency" and what it means to your studies, giving you the chance to better focus your language studying efforts.

Another activity you will consider today to boost your language learning efforts and have fun at the same time is to use movies as a language learning tool.

Most people already enjoy watching movies in their native language so it is a simple switch to begin watching some movies in the language you are studying. Not only will this improve your listening comprehension but you may learn a few words along the way. Additionally, you can use movies for active study by keeping a piece of paper and pen while you watch it and noting down any words that you want to learn for later.

Additionally, if you have already seen a movie in English and have the movie on DVD, you may have the chance of switching the movie into the language you are studying. Since you are already familiar with the plot and what the characters are generally saying, this will give you an added boost in comprehension.

You may try adding subtitles in the foreign language while listening to the English or use English subtitles while listening to the foreign language. However, be careful when doing this because the tendency is to focus solely on the English part and ignore the foreign language. Ultimately, you may find it easier just to keep only one or the other on.

In any case, give movies in your language a try as it can be a powerful learning tool as well as a way to enjoy your language studies.

Today you continued your language studies and considered another enjoyable language resource for the future.

C ongratulations! You have reached Day 30! If you have followed the activities and faithfully studied, you will not only have made excellent progress in your language of choice but you will also have the skills, techniques and tools to help you learn even more of the language in the future.

From now on, you will want to continue each day the language learning habit that you created through this challenge. If you continue each day, there is no way you can fail to reach your goal. As you continue to study, add more resources to your learning and try to think about and test new ideas for learning better and more efficiently. You should always be trying to find a better, quicker and more enjoyable way for yourself to learn your language.

Remember that as long as you continue to study at least a little bit each and every day, you will make progress so that one day you will wake up sometime in the future and realize that you actually know quite a bit in the language you are studying!

Keep using the techniques that you have learned through this 30 day process that work best for you. Also remember that you can always visit: www.learnthatlanguagenow. com to get more information or more help. The forums there are particularly useful if you want to meet other serious language learners and trade tips and tactics. If you have any questions about language learning, you can also ask them in the forum and you will quickly get an answer.

Also, I love to hear feedback from you about your language learning adventures so if you have anything to say, please contact me! You can find my contact information on www.learnthatlanguagenow.com or you can leave a post in the forum, whichever way is easier for you.

Printed in Great Britain
by Amazon